"Sing Me A Story, Read Me A Song"

by
Kathryn L. Cloonan

Illustrated by

Liz Bergstrom • Lori Stevens • George Bacon

Rhythm & Reading Resources
5125 N. Amarillo Drive, Beverly Hills, FL 34465

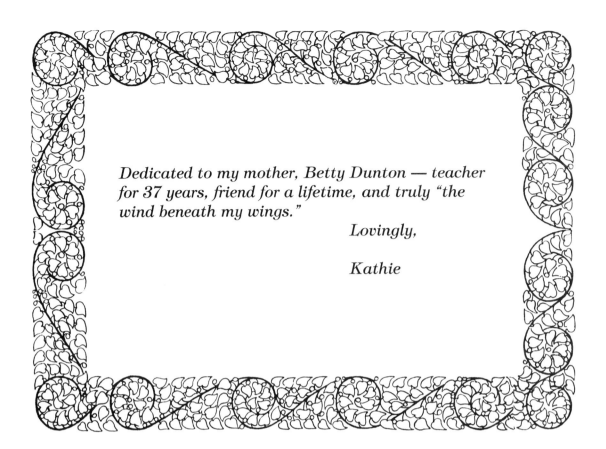

Dedicated to my mother, Betty Dunton — teacher for 37 years, friend for a lifetime, and truly "the wind beneath my wings."

Lovingly,

Kathie

"Sing Me A Story, Read Me A Song"

"SING ME A STORY, READ ME A SONG" is a companion book to Kathryn Cloonan's workshop and cassette of favorite children's songs. It is designed

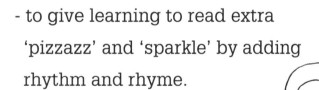

- to give busy teachers easy-to-use ideas and patterns for turning favorite children's songs into Big Books, mini books, and class books.

- to give Music a new place of importance in the classroom...in the Reading corner!

- to give learning to read extra 'pizzazz' and 'sparkle' by adding rhythm and rhyme.

- to give children of all ages and abilities reading successes they can sing about!

Table of Contents

Table of Contents

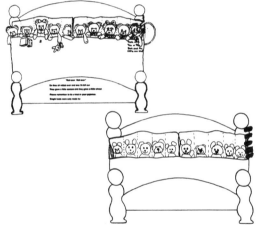

Introduction

Putting songs into print helps children make that vital connection between what they say/sing and what they see in written form. The predictability of a familiar verse gives children the security necessary to take the risk to read.

Songs and chants — filled with rhythm, rhyme and repetition — also offer young readers a supportive reading structure in which they can find success. These elements of rhythm, rhyme and repetition make verses easy to read and easy to remember. In addition, songs and chants offer a combination of predictability and meaningful context so important to children who are trying out early decoding strategies.

By their very nature, the verses of these songs and chants give children lots of repetition of basic sight words that they will come across in written literature. Words such as "the," "is," "was," "in," & "and" make up 80 percent of all **printed** language but are difficult to learn out of context. Songs reinforce these heavy-duty words through their extremely high frequency of use and enrich sight vocabularies with more colorful words as well.

So...move over "Dick and Jane," songs are here to fill the hands and hearts of young <u>Readers</u> everywhere!!

Steps

SING IT — Sing lots of songs often.

PRINT IT — Print a favorite song on chart paper.

READ IT — Read chart and let children read it. Use chart as a springboard for teaching reading concepts and skills.

MAKE IT — Use *"Sing Me A Story, Read Me A Song"* ideas and patterns to make a Big Book, mini books, or class book.

ILLUSTRATE IT — Have children illustrate it.

READ IT — Read it and encourage children to read it. Use these books as a springboard to other reading successes!!

BINGO

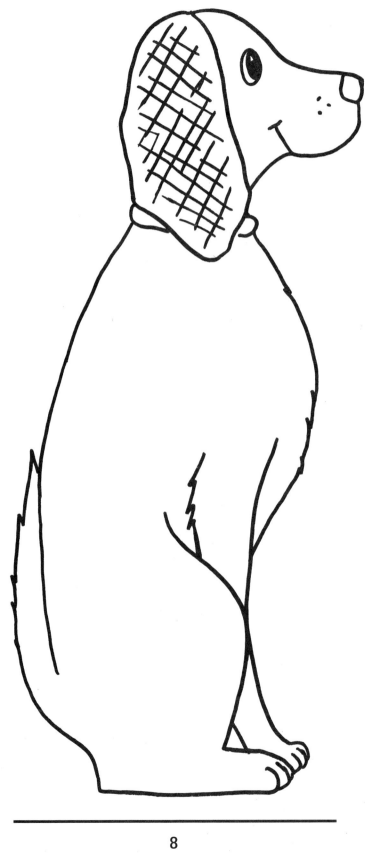

BINGO

Lyrics   *There was a farmer had a dog*

Part A   *And Bingo was his name-o!*

Part B
> *B. I. N. G. O.*
> *B. I. N. G. O.*
> *B. I. N. G. O.*
> *And Bingo was his name-o!*

Big Book is made in the shape of a dog. Pages are of white poster board. Black ears of velour paper add "touchability" to Bingo. After singing/reading the whole song through once, the last letter of Bingo is left off and replaced with a dog bark. Each verse thereafter leaves off one additional letter until Bingo is spelled entirely in dog barks. To show this in the Big Book, a paw print is stamped over the letters to be replaced with dog barks.

Materials For Big Book:
> 4 white poster boards 22"x28"
> 1 sheet of black velour paper 8"x11"
> large paw print stamp & stamp pad
> book bindings or rings
> black magic marker, scissors
> white glue

BINGO

Directions For Big Book:

1. Using pattern* on page 8, enlarge Bingo until he is approx. $20\frac{1}{2}$" tall.

2. Trace onto white poster board 2 Bingos/per sheet of 22"x28" poster board.

3. Trace and cut out 7 Bingos in all.

4. Still using enlarged Bingo, trace 1 ear on extra piece of paper for a pattern.

5. Using this pattern, cut out two ears from black velour paper or black construction paper.

6. Glue ears on front and back cover with white glue.

7. On back (flip side) of each Bingo write part A of verse.

8. On the front side of each Bingo (except cover) write part B of verse. Space letters **B,I,N,G,O** approx. 1" apart.

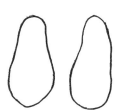

Write part A of verse →   ← Write part B of verse

9. Use large paw print stamp to stamp over the **O's** on the second page that has part B of the verse. **BING**

10. On the third page that has part B of the verse, stamp over the **G & O's.** **BIN**

11. Continue stamping over one more letter on each page that has part B of the verse. The last page has all the letters **B,I,N,G,O** stamped over.

12. Bind.

---

*Transparency available in Transparency Kit; see page 65.

Bingo

Mini books are made up of seven dog shaped pages. The format of singing/reading the whole song through once and then replacing the last letter on the next verse with a dog bark is the same as in the Big Book. The next verses each replace one additional letter with a dog bark until part B of the last page is all done in "barks." The places to "bark" are shown by a paw stamp on the letters.

Materials for mini books:

> 7- 11"x14" brown construction paper
> 3 - $8\frac{1}{2}$"x11" white ditto paper
> scissors, stapler/staples, glue, mini paw stamp/stamp pad, black velour paper-optional

Directions for mini books:

1. Enlarge pattern on page 12 to fit 11"x14" paper.
2. Thermofax enlarged pattern and run off seven 11"x14" Bingos on brown construction paper.
3. Cut out these seven Bingos.

4. Using master on page 13, run off 2 pages of verses on white ditto paper (per mini book).
5. Cut along dotted lines on verse pages.
6. Glue verses to 6 Bingos.
7. Leave seventh Bingo for cover.

8. Leave first Bingo page with verse on it as is.
9. On second page with verse, use mini paw stamp and stamp over o's in part B of verse.
10. On third page with verse stamp over g,o's.
11. On fourth page with verse stamp over n,g,o's.
12. On fifth page with verse stamp i,n,g,o's.
13. On sixth page with verse stamp B,i,n,g,o's.
14. Add cover and staple pages together. Illustrate. Add two black velour ears-optional.

Enlarge to fit on 11"x14" paper
for Bingo mini books

There was a farmer had a dog

And Bingo was his name-o!

B. i. n. g. o.

B. i. n. g. o.

B. i. n. g. o.

And Bingo was his name-o!

• •

There was a farmer had a dog

And Bingo was his name-o!

B. i. n. g. o.

B. i. n. g. o.

B. i. n. g. o.

And Bingo was his name-o!

• •

There was a farmer had a dog

And Bingo was his name-o!

B. i. n. g. o.

B. i. n. g. o.

B. i. n. g. o.

And Bingo was his name-o!

Hickory, Dickory, Dock

Hickory, Dickory, Dock

Lyrics:
Hickory, dickory, dock.

The mouse ran up the clock.

The clock struck <u>one</u>.

The mouse ran down.

Hickory, dickory, dock.

Big Book is made in the shape of a 'grandfather' clock. Hands on clock face turn to integrate telling time. Mouse climbs up and down side of clock on flat ribbon.

Materials for Big Book:
    1 - 22"x14" brown poster board or white poster board
        covered with brown butcher paper
    1 paper clock face and hands (often found in back of
        math workbooks)
    1 - 4"x4" sheet of brown velour art paper
    flat ribbon ($\frac{1}{4}$" x approx. 26") or yarn
    7 sheets of heavy paper 7"x10"
    1 index card
    2 brads/fasteners
    stapler, brown magic marker, scissors

Directions for Big Book:
1. Using pattern* on page 14, enlarge grandfather clock to approx. 22"x14". Trace onto brown poster board (or brown butcher paper glued on white poster board).
2. Cut out.
3. Add paper clock face to top section.
4. Attach hands with brad/fastener.
5. Staple 6 pieces of heavy paper 7"x10" to lower section of grandfather clock.

*Transparency available in Transparency Kit.

Hickory, Dickory, Dock

6. Decorate top page like pendulum and weights.

7. Write one line of verse on each following page.

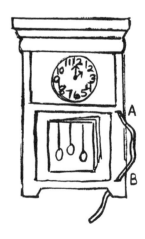

8. On page with words, "the clock struck <u>one</u>":

    a. cut out small window near right edge

    b. cut a 6" circle from extra sheet of heavy paper

    c. attach to back of page with brad

    d. write numbers 1-12 in window

9. Using pattern on this page, cut one mouse out of brown velour art paper and one out of index card.

10. Staple mouse cut out of index card on 26" long flat ribbon.

11. Glue velour mouse on top of mouse cut out of index card for added support.

12. Make $\frac{1}{4}$" cut at points A and B.

13. Thread ribbon through points A and B and tie in the back.

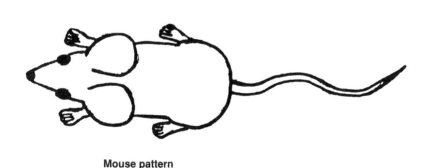

Mouse pattern

Happy Birthday

HAPPY BIRTHDAY!

Happy Birthday

Lyrics: *Happy Birthday to you!*

Happy Birthday to you!

Happy Birthday dear _____!

Happy Birthday to you!

Big Book is made in the shape of a cake. Decorations are done with glitter and real birthday candles. Last page has room for all the children in the class to sign it.

Materials

2 pieces of poster board
glitter
glue
scissors, magic markers or crayons
birthday candles
tape, stapler or book binding

Directions for Big Book:

1. Make 4 cake shaped pages by enlarging cake pattern* on page 17 onto poster board to approx. 22"x14" each. Cut out each cake.

2. Write "Happy Birthday" on front cover.

3. Decorate cover and add glitter.

4. With paper punch, make holes for candles near top of cover. Insert candles and secure with tape on back side of cover.

5. Write one line of verse on each inside page.

6. On last page write "From" and have each child in the class sign it.

7. Staple or bind together.

*Transparency available in Transparency Kit.

Happy Birthday

Mini books are made in the shape of a cake. Each child has a mini book with real candles to show how old he/she is in September. Mini books are decorated with crayons and glitter. Mini books can be hung up at the beginning of the year and used as a bulletin board decoration. On a child's birthday, his/her cake is taken down and one more candle is added. Then everyone in the class signs it and/or writes a little message.

Materials for mini books:

pink, brown, white construction paper $8\frac{1}{2}$"x11"

thermofax

white ditto paper

glitter & glue

paper punch, crayons, scissors, stapler/staples

Directions for mini books:

1. Make a thermofax or ditto of cake page 21.

2. Run off birthday cakes on pink, brown, and white construction paper (so children can choose "chocolate, vanilla or cherry" cakes).

3. Fold cake page in half to make "cake book."

4. Make thermofax or ditto of verses on pages 22 and 23.

5. Run off verses front-to-back on ditto paper.

6. Fold pages together so verses are in the right order.

Happy Birthday

7. Insert verses into construction paper cake book.

8. Cut along top edge of cake to round off and make book more "cake-shaped."

9. Let children choose cover and decorate with crayons, markers and glitter.

10. Staple pages inside. Write "From:" on inside of back cover.

11. Write child's name on "Happy Birthday dear_____" page.

12. On cover, use paper punch to make holes for candles.

13. Stick candles through holes and secure with tape to back.

14. Write child's name and birthdate along bottom of front cover.

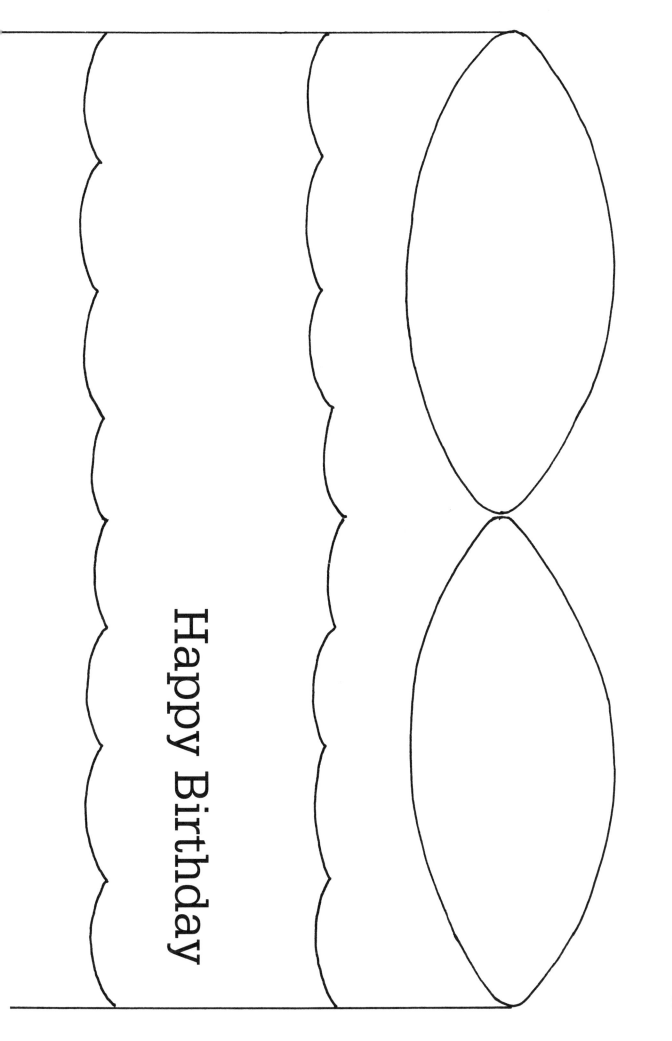

Happy Birthday

Happy Birthday to you!   Happy Birthday to you!

Happy Birthday to you!

Happy Birthday, dear _____

We Have a Friend

Lyrics: *We have a friend*

And her name is <u>Amy</u>.

<u>Amy</u> is her name.

Hello, <u>Amy</u>

Hello, <u>Amy</u>

Hello, <u>Amy</u>

We're so glad you're here!

Innovation I - Change name of child

Innovation II - Change second part of verse to:

Good-bye, <u>Amy</u>

Good-bye, <u>Amy</u>

Good-bye, <u>Amy</u>

We'll see you tomorrow!

Big Book is made in the shape of children. Each page is a different child in the class. The children use patterns to cut "clothes" from wallpaper books or construction paper for their page. "Hello" lyrics are written on the front of each page. "Good-bye" lyrics are written on the back of each page.

We Have a Friend

Materials For Big Book:

Oak tag paper - 12"x18"/per child

Oak tag paper to make patterns

Wallpaper and/or construction paper

scissors, glue

yarn, buttons - optional

Directions for Big Book:

1. Enlarge pattern* on page 28 to approx. 18" tall.

2. Make or have children make one oak tag person per child.

3. On oak tag, make duplicate patterns of tee shirt, pants, and skirt from pages 29 and 30.

4. Let children use these patterns to make clothes to "dress" their oak tag person.

5. Children can trace clothes patterns on wallpaper or construction paper and cut them out. (One set of clothes for front and one set of clothes for back).

6. Glue paper clothes to oak tag person with white glue.

7. Yarn and buttons can be added for hair and eyes.

8. Write "Hello" verse on front of each child's oak tag person using their name.

9. Write "Good-bye" verse on the back of each one.

*Transparency is available in Transparency Kit

We Have a Friend

Mini books are made up of one page for each child in class. Individual verses are written on each page by inserting a different child's name on each one. Children illustrate each page by drawing a picture of the person named on that page. We usually include optional pages for Mom and Dad depending on each individual child's situation.

Materials for mini books:

2—8½"x11" colored construction paper/child

ditto paper-1 piece/child in book

thermofax

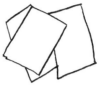

Directions for mini books:

1. Using master on page 31, xerox 1 copy/child.
2. Fill in one child's name in blanks on each xeroxed page (or let children write in their own names).
3. Make thermofax of each page.
4. Run off and collate so each child receives a book with a page about each one of his classmates.
5. Staple together with a front and back construction paper cover.
6. Let children draw a picture of each one of their classmates on bottom of appropriate pages and decorate cover.

*** Some computer programs such as MECC's "Letters, Labels & Lists" have mail-merge capacities in which they will automatically insert each name on a list into a verse.

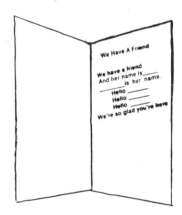

Enlarge to approx. 18" tall

28

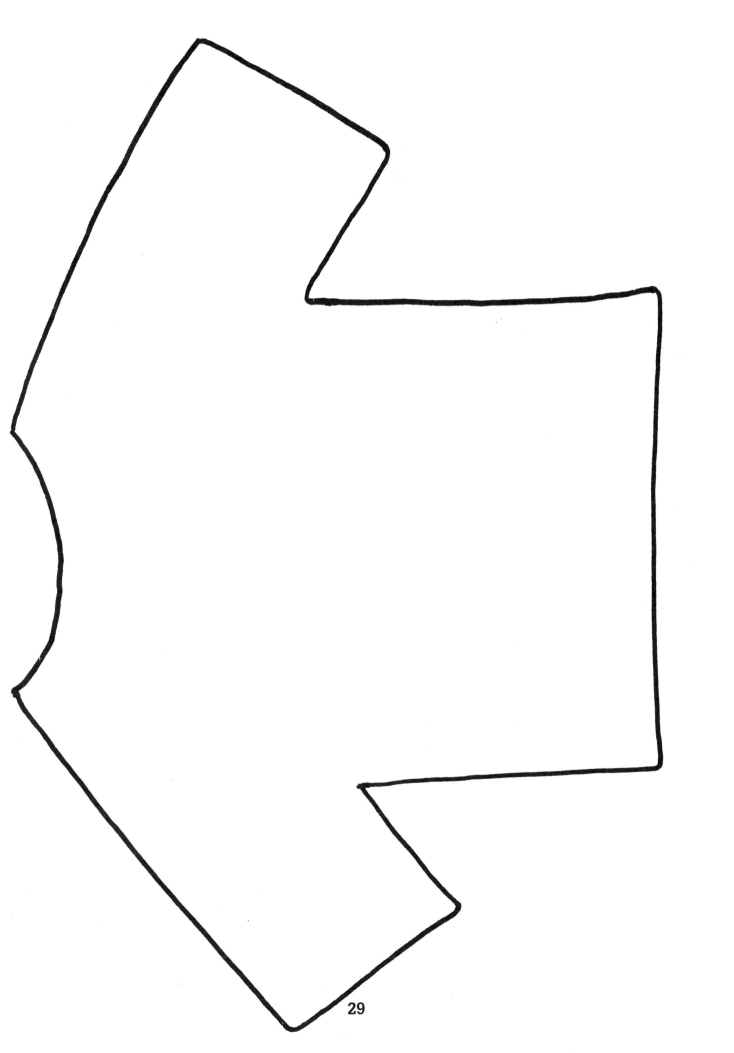

29

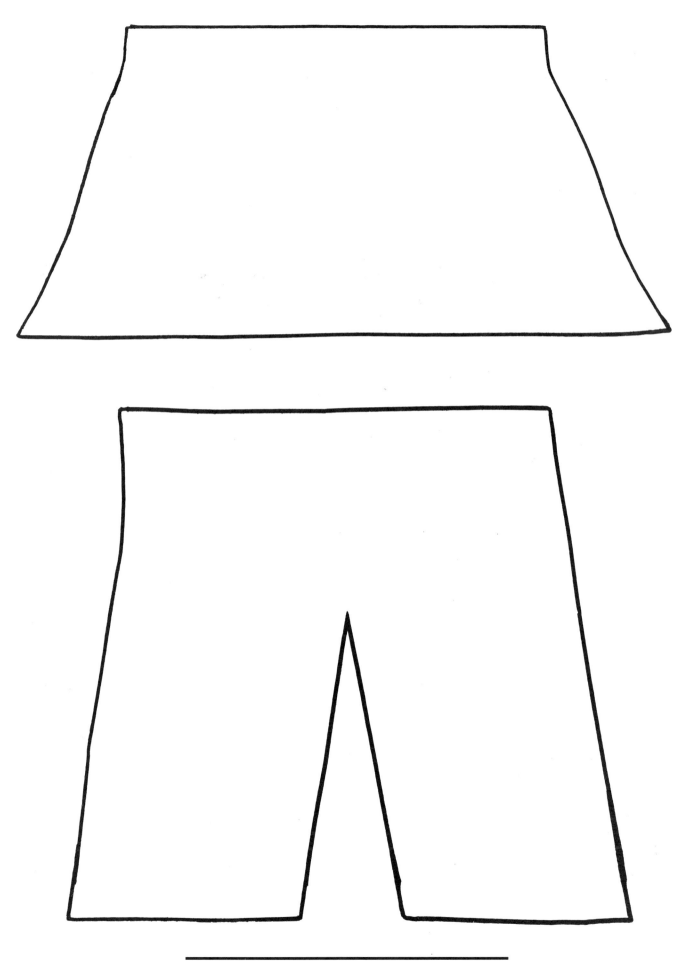

30

We Have a Friend

We have a friend

And ___ name is_____
   his/her

_____ is ___ name
                    his/her

Hello _____

Hello _____

Hello _____

We're so glad you're here

Little Skunk

Little Skunk

Lyrics:

Little Skunk's Hole

Oh! I stuck my head in a little skunk's hole
And the little skunk said, "God bless your soul!"
　　Take it out!
　　Take it out!
　　Take it out!
　　Remove it!

But I didn't take it out and the little skunk said,
"If you don't take it out, you'll wish you had!"
　　Take it out!
　　Take it out!
　　Take it out!
　　PSSSSSSSSSSSSSSSSSSSSSST!
　　I removed it!

Big Book is made in the shape of a log. Verses are on pages attached to length of log. A skunk puppet fits inside log.

Materials:

1　extra large cylinder oatmeal box
4—12"x18" brown construction paper
3—8½"x11" white ditto paper
black marker
rubber cement
stapler/staples
crayons or markers for illustrating
masking tape

skunk puppet

Directions:

1. Attach short side of 12"x18" brown construction paper to oatmeal box with masking tape.

2. Wrap paper around box and secure by stapling or with rubber cement.

Little Skunk

3. Use black marker to draw textured "log" effect.

4. Cut ten $4\frac{1}{2}$"x9" pages from rest of brown construction paper.

5. Cut white ditto paper into ten $3\frac{1}{2}$" x $8\frac{1}{2}$" pages.

6. Using rubber cement, glue white pages onto nine of the brown pages.

7. Write words to song on pages.

8. Have children illustrate pages.

9. Use last piece of $4\frac{1}{2}$"x9" brown paper as cover. Draw textured "log" effect with black marker.

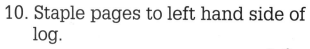

10. Staple pages to left hand side of log.

11. Add skunk and sing!

Michael Finnagin

Michael Finnagin

Lyrics:

There once was man named Michael Finnagin

He had whiskers on his chin-again.

The wind came along and blew them in-again

Poor old Michael Finnagin...begin-again!

There once was a man named Michael Finnagin

He went fishing with a pin-again.

Caught a whale that pulled him in-again.

Poor old Michael Finnagin...begin-again!

There once was a man named Michael Finnagin.

He was fat and then grew thin-again.

Ate so much he had to begin-again.

Poor old Michael Finnagin...begin-again!

Big Book is designed to look like Michael Finnagin with shaggy hair and beard. Removable face allows children to stick their face in opening and "become" Michael Finnagin. Verses to song and children's illustrations look like a pocket on the sweatshirt.

Michael Finnagin

Materials for Big Book:

1 white poster board 14"x22"

1 white poster board $5\frac{1}{2}$"x9"

1 $8\frac{1}{2}$"x11" sheet of black velour paper

1 sheet of fake fur

1 $\frac{1}{2}$"x1" piece of self-sticking velcro (both rough & soft sided parts)

1 small children's gray sweatshirt <u>or</u> gray material 16"x24"

crayons or markers

rubber cement

4 $8\frac{1}{2}$"x11" white construction paper

Directions for Big Book:

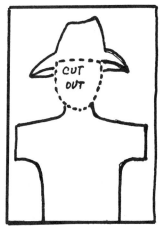

1. Enlarge pattern* on page 40 to approximately 22" high and trace onto 14"x22" white poster board.

2. With markers or crayons, color in details of face.

3. Carefully cut out face oval along dotted line.

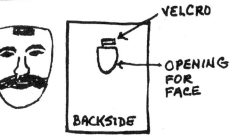

4. Put a small piece of soft-sided velcro at top front of face oval.

5. Put a matching piece of rough-sided velcro on back of poster board so face oval can be attached in place.

6. Lay hair/beard pattern found on page 41 on <u>wrong</u> side of piece of fake fur.

Michael Finnagin

7. Draw around hair/beard pattern onto wrong side of fake fur.

8. Cut along lines drawn.

9. Turn fake fur over and fit around edges of cut-away hole on white poster board. (Hair will hang down approx. 1" at top of oval hole.)

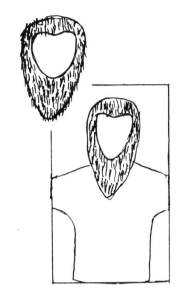

10. Use rubber cement to glue fake fur in place just around edges of cut-out hole and leave beard hanging down freely.

11. Using pattern on page 42 cut hat out of black velour paper.

12. Use rubber cement to glue velour hat in place.

13. Use scraps of fake fur to make moustache and eyebrows.

14. Use rubber cement and glue moustache and eyebrows in place on oval face shape.

15. Use rubber cement and glue small children's sweatshirt in place.

OR

a). Enlarge pattern* on page 43 to approximately 16" across and 14" down.

b.) Trace onto tissue paper.

*Transparency available in Transparency Kit

c.) Use tissue paper pattern and cut sweatshirt out of gray material. Fold edges under all the way around.

d.) Use rubber cement and glue sweatshirt into place.

16. For book part, cut one piece of poster board to $5\frac{1}{2}$"x9".

17. Cut one piece of gray material or scrap material from sweatshirt to $6\frac{1}{2}$"x10".

18. Use rubber cement to glue material onto $5\frac{1}{2}$"x9" poster board for cover. Glue overlapping material to back side of poster board.

19. Cut seven pieces of white construction paper $5\frac{1}{2}$"x$8\frac{1}{2}$".

20. Glue 1 piece of white construction paper to back side of cover.

21. Write or type two lines of song each on rest of pages.

22. Have children illustrate.

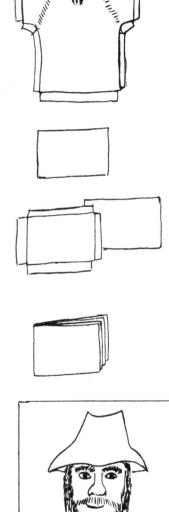

23. Use sewing machine to sew cover and pages onto lower section of sweatshirt on white poster board. (If sewing machine is not avail., use stapler).

Enlarge to approx. 22" high

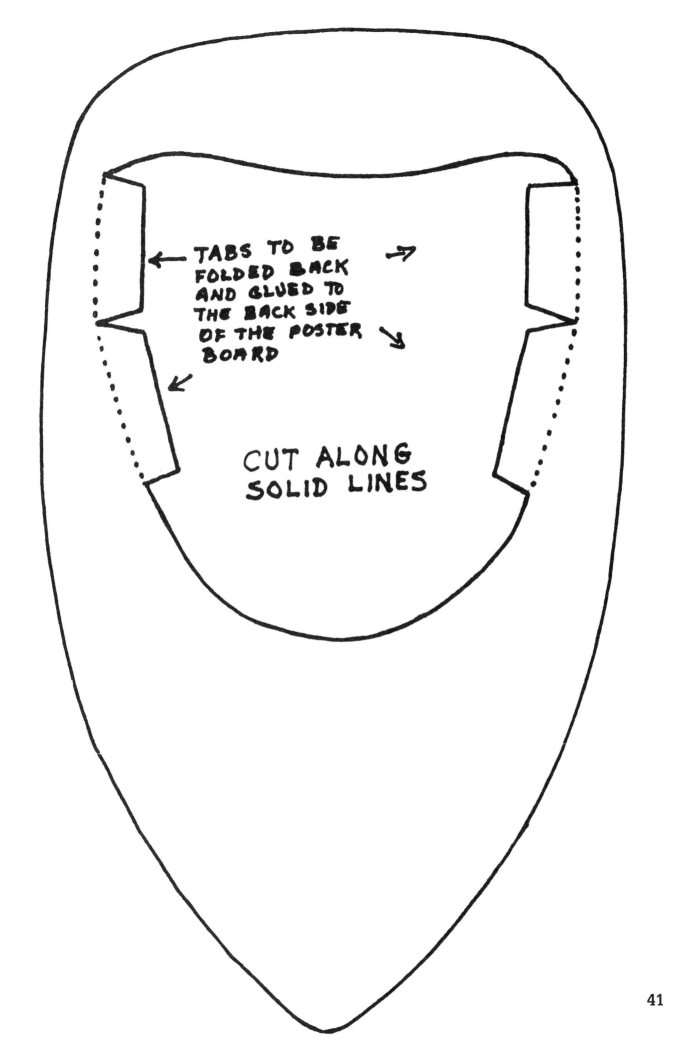

TABS TO BE
FOLDED BACK
AND GLUED TO
THE BACK SIDE
OF THE POSTER
BOARD

CUT ALONG
SOLID LINES

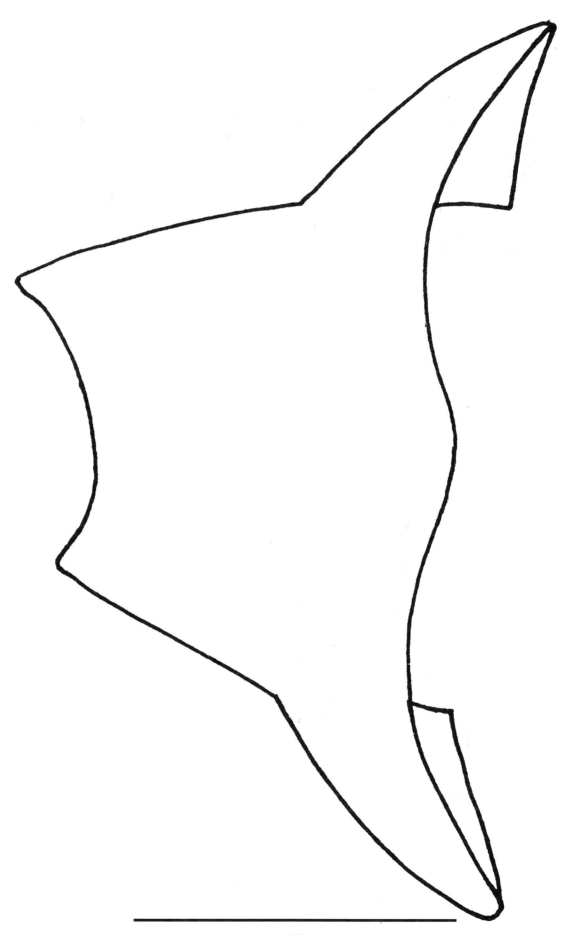

42

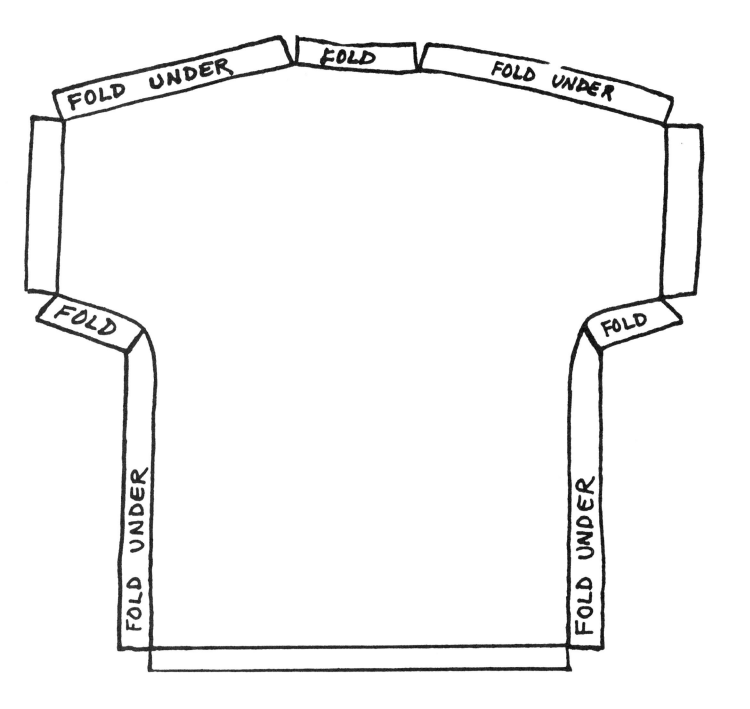

Enlarge to approx. 16" across x 14" down

Ten In The Bed

There were Ten in The Bed and the little one said

"Roll over, Roll over!"

So they all rolled over and one (1) fell out.

They gave a little scream and they gave a little shout...

Please remember to tie a knot in your pajamas...

Single beds were only made for...

Ten In The Bed

Lyrics:

Part A   There were <u>ten</u> in the bed
And the little one said,

Part B   "Roll over, Roll over!"
So they all rolled over and one fell out
And they gave a little scream and they gave a little shout
Please remember to tie a knot in your pajamas
Single beds were only meant for...

nine in the bed and the little one said...(go to part B)
eight, seven, six, five, four, three, two...

Part C   One in the bed and the little one said,

Part D   "I've got the whole mattress to myself!
I've got the whole mattress to myself!
I've got the whole mattress to myself!
I've got the whole mattress to myself!

GOOD-NIGHT!"

Big Book is made in the shape of a big bed filled with ten teddy bears. As each verse is sung, a pillow-shaped page is turned and one more bear falls out of bed. On the last page the little bear has the whole bed to himself.

Materials for Big Book:

1 piece of heavy cardboard 24"x36"

3 pieces of heavy blank chart paper 24"x36"

markers, scissors, glue, stapler/staples, binding

Ten In The Bed

Directions for Big Book:

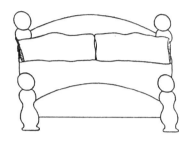

1. Make an overhead transparency of pattern on page 49. Hang one blank sheet of chart paper 24"x36" on the wall.

2. Project transparency onto chart paper so bed is enlarged to $22\frac{1}{4}$"x$30\frac{1}{2}$".

3. Trace bed. **DO NOT** draw in dotted lines.

4. Write part C of verse (see page 45) across the bottom of pillows on bed. Write part D of verse on foot board of bed. Cut out bed.

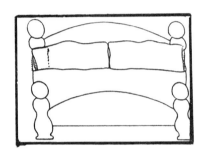

5. Glue bed onto 24"x36" piece of heavy poster board placing right edge of bed very close to right edge of poster board.

6. Using same overhead transparency, trace a second bed (same size as first) onto another sheet of chart paper. Make sure right edge of bed is close to right edge of chart paper. **DO** draw in dotted lines on far left pillow. Leave this bed on wall temporarily.

7. Make overhead transparency of pillow patterns on page 50.

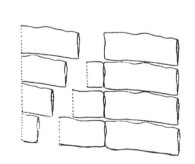

8. Project this transparency onto bed drawing you left hanging on wall (step 6). To make sure pillows are enlarged to the right size, align pillow **#5** with right hand pillow in bed drawing. Matching these carefully will ensure that pillow pages will fit the bed.

9. Take bed drawing off wall. Put up another piece of blank chart paper. Trace pillow pieces (pg. 50) and cut them out.

*Transparency available in Transparency Kit.

Ten In The Bed

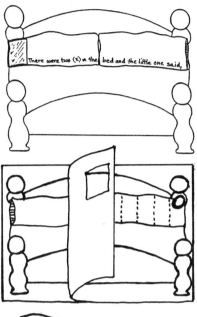

10. Go back to second bed drawing (from step 6) and cut along dotted lines. On this bed drawing write, "There were two (2) in the bed and the little one said," across the bottom of pillows. Write part B of verse (see page 45) on foot board of this bed.

11. To arrange pages, put "One in the bed" page on the bottom. Put "Two in the bed" page on top of it. Put rest of pillow pages in order from largest to smallest with the smallest pillow on the very top.

12. To bind put a grommet* on the right hand side of each page and use a metal ring to hold bed and pillow pages together.

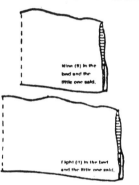

13. Near the bottom of the first page (smallest pillow) write part A of verse (see page 45).

14. For the second pillow page change part A to "Nine in the bed..." and write words far enough to the right that they are hidden when first pillow page is in place.

15. Continue in this manner until each pillow page has a verse written on it.

16. With all the pages in place, draw one bear on each pillow page so there are "Ten in the Bed!"

*Grommets and grommet tool can usually be found in camping/tenting sections of department stores or hardware stores. They come in several sizes, are inexpensive, and really protect Big Books from tearing!!!

Ten In The Bed

Mini book is designed in same manner as big book—
a bed shaped book filled with ten teddy bears. As
each verse is sung, a pillow-shaped page is turned
and one more bear falls out of bed. On the last page
the little bear has the whole bed to himself.

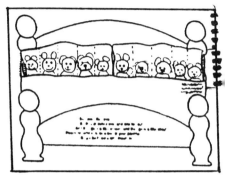

Materials for mini books:

4 pieces of $8\frac{1}{2}$"x14" white paper

scissors, crayons, binding

Directions for mini books:

1. Enlarge masters on pages 51, 52, 53 and 54 to
   each fit $8\frac{1}{2}$"x14" paper (enlarge on copy
   machine by 122%).

2. Run off one of each page per mini book being
   made.

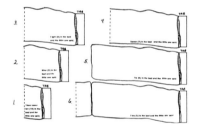

3. Cut along dotted lines on "Two in the bed" page.

4. Cut out pillows on enlarged pillow pages 53 & 54.
   Arrange pillows in a pile from largest to smallest
   with largest on bottom. (Tabs will be on the right
   and dotted lines will be on the left.)

5. Put pillow pages on top of "two in the bed" page
   with right hand edges of all pillow tabs together.
   Put "One in the bed..." page on the bottom.

6. Trim pillow tabs even with edge of paper.

7. Bind all pages together on **right** side and have
   children draw a bear on each pillow.

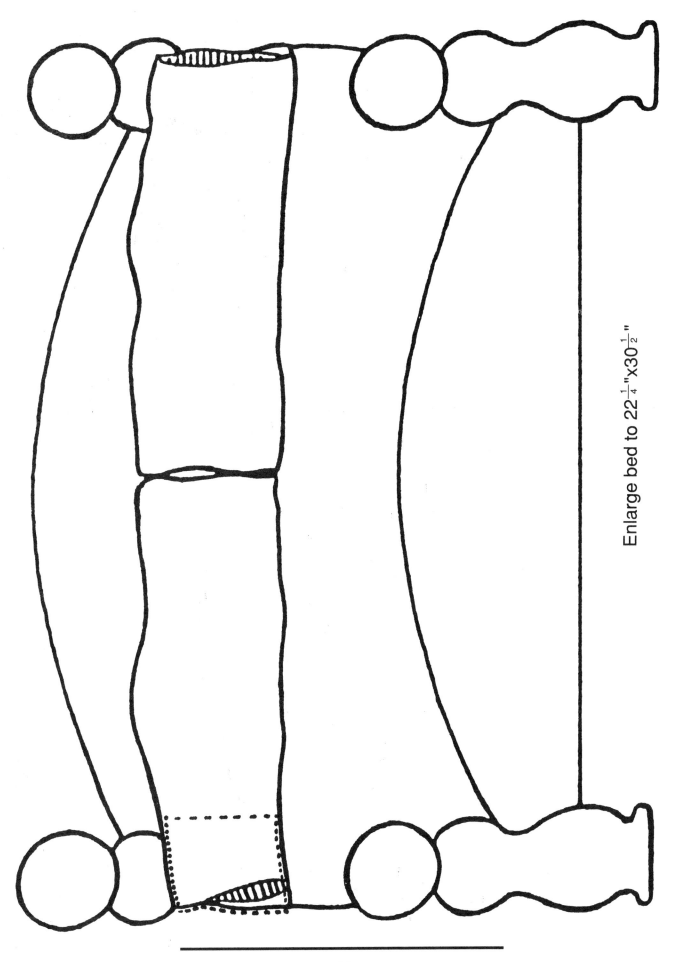

Enlarge bed to $22\frac{1}{4}$"x$30\frac{1}{2}$"

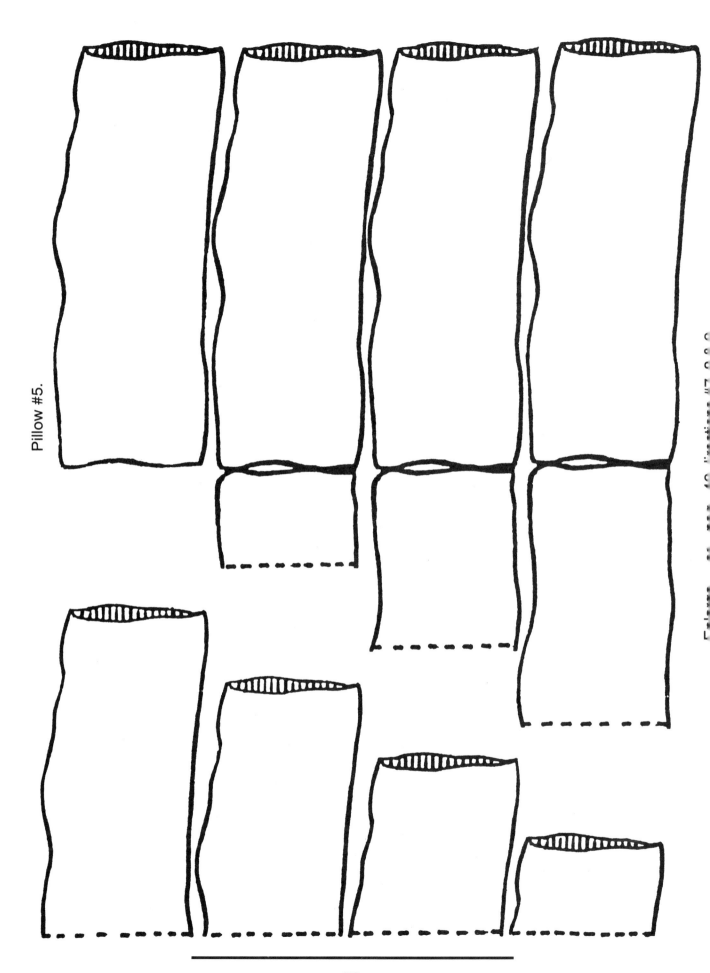

Pillow #5.

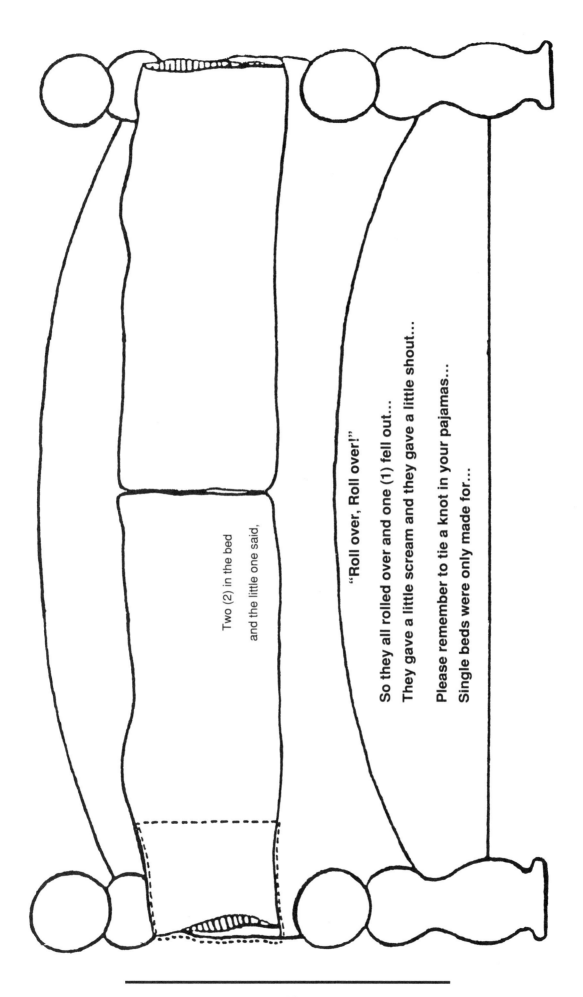

Two (2) in the bed
and the little one said,

"Roll over, Roll over!"

So they all rolled over and one (1) fell out...
They gave a little scream and they gave a little shout...

Please remember to tie a knot in your pajamas...
Single beds were only made for...

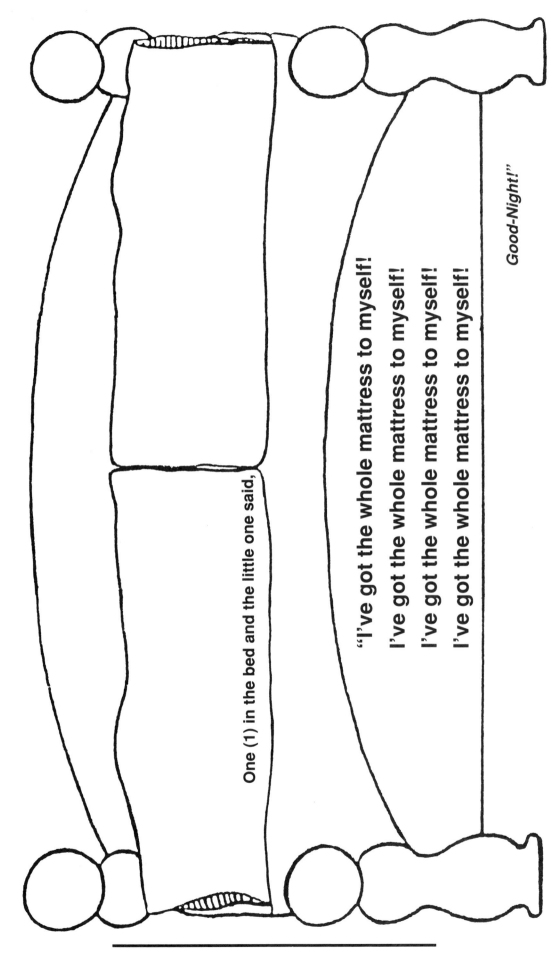

One (1) in the bed and the little one said,

"I've got the whole mattress to myself!
I've got the whole mattress to myself!
I've got the whole mattress to myself!
I've got the whole mattress to myself!

Good-Night!"

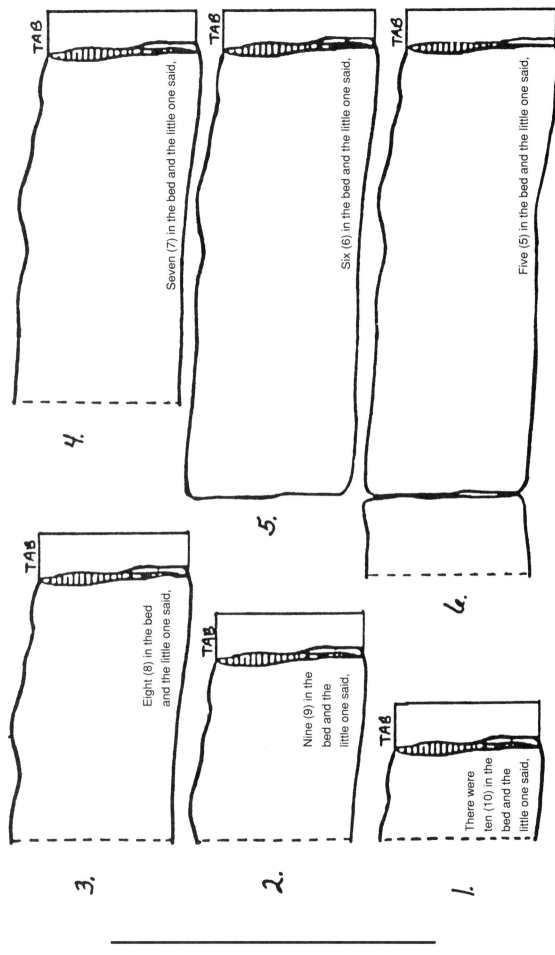

4. TAB

Seven (7) in the bed and the little one said,

5. TAB

Six (6) in the bed and the little one said,

TAB

Five (5) in the bed and the little one said,

6.

3. TAB

Eight (8) in the bed and the little one said,

2. TAB

Nine (9) in the bed and the little one said,

1. TAB

There were ten (10) in the bed and the little one said,

7.

TAB

Four (4) in the bed and the little one said,

8.

TAB

Three (3) in the bed and the little one said,

Dear Boys and Girls,

I hope you enjoy reading and singing lots of songs! Songs have a way of making you smile from the inside out, don't they?

Sometimes teachers and parents need a little extra encouragement to get them to sing along as loudly and cheerfully as you do. Here are some ideas that might help.

(1.) Smile when you notice them singing along.

(2.) Tell them you like their singing.

(3.) Make sure you sing your very best so you can help them remember the tune.

If you have found any other ways to encourage your teacher or parents to sing along more often, please let me know! And I will pass your ideas on to other boys and girls.

I would also love to know what your favorite songs are.

Hope to hear from you soon.

Keep Singing!

Sincerely,

Mrs. Cloonan

Mrs. Cloonan

P.S. It's ok to use your inventive spelling. And remember the nice thing about inventive spelling is you're always right!

5125 N. Amarillo Drive ▪ Beverly Hills, Florida 34465

Resources

Records and Tapes

"Sing Me A Story, Read Me A Song," Kathryn Cloonan
Peter, Paul and Mommy, Peter, Paul & Mary
Elephant Show Record, Sharon, Lois & Bram
Special Delivery, Fred Penner
The Cat Came Back, Fred Penner
Learning Basic Skills Through Music, Hap Palmer
We All Live Together, Volumes 1,2,3, & 4 Greg Scelse & Steve Millang
Doing The Dinosaur Rock, Diane Butchelor, The Learning Line Inc.
You'll Sing A Song And I'll Sing A Song, Ella Jenkins
Singable Songs For The Very Young, Raffi
More Singable Songs For The Very Young, Raffi

Big Books

My Dog, Rigby Education
Sing A Song, Wright Group

Resource Books

"Sing Me A Story, Read Me A Song-Book I, Kathryn Cloonan, Rhythm & Reading Resources, 1991
"Sing Me A Story, Read Me A Song, Book II, Kathryn Cloonan, Rhythm & Reading Resources, 1991
A Song Is A Rainbow, Zeittin, Patty, Scott Foresman and Co., 1982
Piggyback Books, Jean Warren, Warren Publishing House, Inc., 1988
Kids Songs, Nancy & John Cassidy, Klutz Press, 1986
World's Best Funny Songs, Esther Nelson, Sterling Publishing Co., 1988

Transparency Kit for *"Sing Me A Story, Read Me A Song" Book 1*
8 transparencies $4.95 + $1.00 shipping & handling, send to:

RHYTHM & READING RESOURCES
5125 N. Amarillo Drive, Beverly Hills, FL 34465